B.C.
Great Zot, I'm Beautiful

by
Johnny Hart

A FAWCETT GOLD MEDAL BOOK
Fawcett Publications, Inc., Greenwich, Connecticut

I'D LIKE ONE TICKET TO THE BEACH.
TICKETS
IS THAT THE OUTFIT YOU'RE WEARING?
YES.
6·18
SOLD OUT

7.2

"RING."

NO, SHE'S NOT HERE RIGHT NOW, THIS IS HER GIRLFRIEND.

... WHAT DO I LOOK LIKE? ... WHY DON'T YOU COME OVER AND SEE, BIG BOY?

7-9

WHOOPS

ZIP

☼ SIGH......
ALMOST MADE IT TO THE CREST OF THE HILL.

7·10

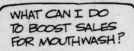

7.19

7·21

7-22

ig·nite' v.

the evening of the
annual IG festival.

7·24

7:26

7-27

THANKS FOR THE NEAT 'TAKE'.

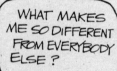

7-29

7·30

8-2

8-7

SLUURP

8-9

BE SURE TO TUNE IN TOMORROW FOR A MAMMOTH AARRGGHH.

AAAA
RRGGHHH

8·10

hart

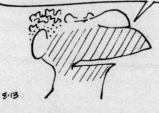

8·13

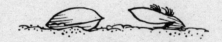

8-17

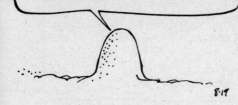

8-21

ZOT

AAAAGGH

8-27

9.2

9.3

9.4

9.6

9.10

9·11

9·22

9.27

9-30

THERE MUST BE SOME
REASON WHY WE'RE
HERE.

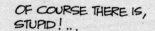

OF COURSE THERE IS,
STUPID! ...

10·4

WE'RE HERE TO
PROLIFERATE
THE SPECIES!

LET'S LEAVE THE I.R.S.
OUT OF THIS! ....WHY
ARE WE **REALLY** HERE?

10·11

10·18

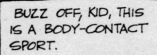

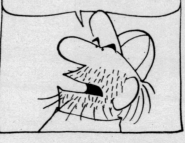

. . . . . .

10-19

10-20

10·22

11-2

11·5

11·8

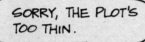

11·9

YOU'RE LATEST BOOK LOOKS GREAT!

HOW DO YOU WRITERS COME UP WITH THOSE FANTASTIC IDEAS?

PETER'S PUBLISHING CO.

11-11

LIKE, I MEAN, WHO WOULD EVER THINK OF PUTTING A LAME-BRAINED IDIOT IN CHARGE OF A PUBLISHING COMPAN......

11·15

YOU LEFT OUT THE "B".

WHAT ARE YOU DOING?

I'M GOING TO BURN THESE LEAVES.

...AND POLLUTE THE AIR?... YOU SHOULD BE ASHAMED OF YOURSELF!

11-17

BY GOLLY, THE RED ONES AREN'T HALF BAD!

ZANG

11·22

CHOP CHOP
CHOP
CHIP CHIP
CHOP CHIP
CHOP CHOP
CHOP

11·30